— MASTERING THE ART OF —
GOAL SETTING

Learn Strategies to Skyrocket Your Efficiency, Embrace Personal Development, and Accomplish More in Less Time

by

J P PATHAK

Email: jppathak1@gmail.com

Copyright © 2024 by J P Pathak

All rights reserved. No part of this book may be reproduced in any form without permission in writing from the author.

No part of this publication may be reproduced or transmitted in any form or by any means, mechanical or electronic, including photocopying or recording, by any information storage and retrieval system, or by email or any other means whatsoever without permission in writing from the author.

DEDICATION

To my loving wife, **Meera**,

Your unconditional support and boundless love have been the cornerstone of my journey towards mastering the art of goal setting. Your strength, resilience, and determination in setting and achieving your own goal have been an inspiration to me, our daughters, **'Juhi and Garima',** and our little angels, **'Ridhhima and Yashika.'**

Thank you for being my rock, my confidence, and my biggest cheerleader. This book, 'Mastering The Art of Goal Setting' is dedicated to you.

With Love and Gratitude.

- J P Pathak

ACKNOWLEDGMENT

I extend my deepest gratitude to my remarkable colleagues whose unwavering collaboration has infused every moment of this writing endeavor with joy and inspiration. This book is a reflection of our united voyage, a testament to our collective effort.

Your combined wisdom, camaraderie, and shared encounters have elevated my existence in immeasurable ways, transforming my journey into an unforgettable odyssey.

Special appreciation to **Mr. Som Bathala,** my invaluable coach and mentor, whose guidance propelled me forward with unwavering encouragement. I am also indebted to **Mr. Ravi Tewari,** my esteemed editor, whose insights and expertise have been instrumental in shaping this book.

- J P Pathak

WHY IS THIS BOOK FOR YOU?

In "Mastering the Art of Goal Setting," JP Pathak unveils a transformative roadmap to harnessing the immense power of goal setting and personal evolution. Seamlessly weaving together ancient Indian wisdom and contemporary insights from psychology and leadership, this book serves as your indispensable toolkit for unleashing your boundless potential and realizing your deepest aspirations.

Prepare to embark on an exhilarating journey of self-discovery and empowerment as you delve into the pages of this comprehensive guide.

Through riveting narratives, illuminating anecdotes, and immersive exercises, you'll learn to:

- Craft crystal-clear goals that resonate with your core values and boldest dreams.
- Forge actionable strategies to overcome obstacles and triumphantly attain your objectives.
- Cultivate an unwavering sense of motivation, resilience, and determination to fuel your pursuit of greatness.

- Master the art of intention, commitment, and focused action to manifest your most audacious visions into reality.

"Mastering the Art of Goal Setting" isn't just a book—it's a beacon of inspiration and guidance for those who dare to dream big and strive for excellence.

With the timeless wisdom of *Ramdas* and the sage counsel of his *Guru Ji,* coupled with captivating storytelling, this masterpiece is an indispensable resource for anyone poised to unlock their inner potential and sculpt a life brimming with purpose, passion, and boundless possibility.

Prepare to be stirred, motivated, and propelled toward your greatest aspirations as you immerse yourself in the pages of this transformative work.

TABLE OF CONTENTS

INTRODUCTION 13

THE FOUNDATION OF GOAL SETTING 19

    IMPORTANCE OF GOAL SETTING 21

    STORYTIME 22

    EXERCISE 23

STRATEGIC PLANNING FOR SUCCESS 27

SMART GOAL FRAMEWORK 31

    EXERCISE: NO 1 37

    EXERCISE: NO 2 38

    EXERCISE 40

ALIGNING INDIVIDUAL AND TEAM GOALS 41

    ENCOURAGING COLLABORATION IN GOAL-SETTING 41

    EXERCISE 46

    EXERCISE 48

    KEY CONSIDERATIONS 48

ADOPTING GOALS TO CHANGING ENVIRONMENT 51

    NAVIGATING CHALLENGES AND UNCERTAINTIES IN GOAL SETTING 51

    PESTLE ANALYSIS 52

    SWOT ANALYSIS 53

    EXERCISE 54

    MARKET TRENDS 55

    KEY LEARNINGS 56

SUCCESS STORY & THE TRUE POWER OF RESILIENCE 59

STORYTIME 59

LEADERSHIP'S ROLE IN GOAL ATTAINMENT 61

HOW LEADERS CAN INFLUENCE GOAL-SETTING PROCESSES 61

EXERCISE 63

STORYTIME 66

MORAL OF THE STORY 67

EXERCISE 68

EFFECTIVE COMMUNICATION FOR GOAL ACHIEVEMENT 69

ENCOURAGING OPEN DIALOGUES WITHIN A TEAM 69

WHAT IS EFFECTIVE COMMUNICATION? 69

STORYTIME 71

STORYTIME 73

LESSON LEARNED 75

EXERCISE 75

MEASURING AND CELEBRATING SUCCESS 77

STORYTIME 79

THE LESSON I LEARNED 85

EXERCISE 85

CASE STUDY 86

EXERCISE 90

LEARNING FROM FAILURE 91

KEY LESSONS LEARNED 91

AN UNSTEADY START 91

SUSTAINING MOTIVATION 97

MAINTAINING ENTHUSIASM TO SUSTAIN LONG-TERM MOTIVATION 97
FINDING THE PURPOSE IN ADVERSITY 100
GOAL SETTING 102
STORYTIME 103
EXERCISE - REFLECTIVE GOAL-SETTING 108
FINAL THOUGHTS 108

ABOUT THE AUTHOR 111
DISCLAIMER 113
MAY I ASK YOU A FAVOR? 115

INTRODUCTION

"Our goals can only be reached through a vehicle of a plan, in which we must fervently believe, and upon which we must vigorously act. There is no other route to success."

- Stephen A. Brennan

It was a vibrant day in our village, just days before the much-anticipated Holi festival when I witnessed a scene that would shape my understanding of leadership and goal-setting forever as the villagers gathered to discuss the preparations for the colorful festivities. I observed with keen interest. The air was filled with excitement and anticipation, but beneath the surface, there lingered a sense of uncertainty. Despite spirited discussions and heartfelt debates, a crucial decision remains unsolved –the village lacked a strong leader to guide them through the preparation.

In the moment of collective realization, the villagers turned to an unexpected source of guidance father, fondly referred to as Guru Ji. With the plea of leadership echoing in the air, they sought his wisdom and insight. Little did I know that this simple request would ignite within me a lifelong journey of discovery, culminating in the mastery of the art of goal-setting.

As the villagers approached my father, seeking guidance on their leadership dilemma, little did they anticipate the unconventional lesson that awaited them. With characteristic wisdom, my father responded to their plea with a seemingly puzzling request; Bring me a bag of peanuts and beans mixed in the same bag"

The villagers were curious and intrigued when they received a request from my father, Guru Ji. He asked them to sort peanuts and beans separately in the village square. However, there was a catch - they had to do it without anyone watching them. The villagers were eager to prove themselves and embarked on the task with fervor. But soon, they realized that it was impossible to sort the peanuts and beans without detection. They returned to Guru Ji, humbled and perplexed. Seeking clarity from my father, they admitted their failure.

With a knowing smile, Guru Ji imparted a timeless lesson on leadership. He said that leadership is akin to sorting peanuts and beans. It's not about performing when others are watching; it's about doing the right things even when no one is watching. A true leader acts with integrity and leads by example, whether in the spotlight or behind the scenes.

In that moment, I gained a profound insight into the essence of leadership - an understanding rooted in integrity, humility, and unwavering commitment to doing what is right. Through this simple yet profound analogy, I learned that the path to true leadership lies not in the pursuit of recognition or visibility, but in the steadfast adherence to principles that guide and inspire others. Let me remind you that my father was addressed as Guru Ji in my village. I have talked about the same in the 1st episode of my series "Rise and Thrive".

Ramdas is a central character and will continue to be our guide in this episode as well like he was in the previous 3 episodes- **"The One Thing, How to Go Beyond Strength, and Mastering The Art of Rise Together"**

Ramdas was elected as the leader. Ramdas found his inspiration from stories my father used to tell to us. There was one such story, Tenali Rama, who was the advisor to the king Krishnadevaraya in the kingdom of Vijaynagaram, faced a royal challenge where he had to meet the king's ambitious goals within a short timeframe. Through strategic, planning, Tenali Rama not only met the objectives but exceeded them, showcasing the power of effective goal setting. As Ramdas reflects on Tenali Rama's clever approach to challenges, he begins to implement similar principles in his own life. The story catalyzes Ramdas's journey into mastering the art of goal setting, setting the stage for the insightful discussions that follow in the book.

Let me share glimpses of episode 1, episode 2, and episode 3, so you are not missing the link, here we go-

In episode 1, **"The One Thing- That Will Make You an Effective Leader**." we saw how Ramdas helped us learn from the wisdom of his Guru Ji. We learned the core elements of exceptional leadership. He was focused on the philosophy of identifying and mastering the singular element that can transform one's leadership capabilities. "The One Thing"- the 1st book in this series has key principles such as prioritization, goal setting, and strategic decision making, all geared towards honing effective leadership skills. The book " The One Thing"- has engaging anecdotes and real-world examples that can propel leaders toward leadership excellence.

In episode 2- "**How to Go Beyond Strength**," we have key themes such as goal setting, problem-solving, positive thinking, success, happiness, and the pivotal role of information in achieving success.

We can draw inspiration from the story shared by Dr. A.P.J Abdul Kalam, former President of India; "The real power of Inspiration." The narrative concludes with another story from a classmate of Rahul Dravid, the coach of the Indian Cricket team- offering an excellent example of resilience, determination, and the transformative impact of these principles on real-life success stories.

The journey begins with "The One Thing", that will make you an effective Leader, Ramdas shares timeless wisdom, drawing from his personal experiences. Against the backdrop of shared goals and aspirations, the narrative takes us detour into a small village fair, where the transformative impact of inclusivity unfolds. There are stories around 'Rising Together' and these tales highlight the strength that lies in unity and the magic that happens when individuals align their aspirations for a common cause.

As the pages turn, the exploration deepens with 'How to Go Beyond Strength', a profound journey into breaking through limits, Of course, Ramdas and his Guru Ji with his characteristic wisdom, lead us through stories of resilience and determination, urging them to discover their untapped potential. The narrative is rich with examples that resonate with the universal struggles and triumphs of the human spirit. We have understood the SOAR a technique to identify the strengths of each team member, opportunities available within the industry to grow, aspirations of team members, and how to measure results. The role of a leader in building a team is one of the highlights of episode 2. You have found this episode as a blueprint for success.

In episode 3- "**Mastering The Art of Rising Together**"

We have discussed the transformative journey towards effective leadership. The central theme revolves around the concept of effective leadership. What will make you an effective leader? It can be Strategic planning for some. Goal setting for others or it can be Self-Esteem, effective communication, or team building. Ramdas, as the insightful guide, facilitates a deep exploration of these diverse facets of leadership.

Ramdas continues to be the guiding force and helped inspire us to develop a balanced leadership style and shares remarkable stories of leaders such as Dr. K. Anji Reddy, Kiran Mazumdar Shaw, Pankaj Patel, RC Bhargava to name a few. Each name unfolds like a masterclass, presenting different leadership styles, from transformative to transactional, inspiring readers to find their unique leadership signature.

The heartbeat: the exploration of 'achieving heights' as one is the heartbeat of this book. Life is a challenging journey that requires us to climb mountains. We can climb any height with the help of each other. In this chapter, we have learned what to avoid. The real meaning of 3 keywords in personal and professional life-

Let us begin our journey to Goal Setting which will start with the foundation of Goal Setting.

THE FOUNDATION OF GOAL SETTING

"Setting goals is the first step in turning the invisible into the visible."

- Tony Robbins (American Author and Coach)

When villagers were talking about preparations for the Holi celebration after accepting their defeat and selected Ramdas as their 'hero a true leader in action'.

Guru Ji brought a seed and asked the people there, what is this seed holding within? there were many responses, like protein, life, water, and so on. Guru Ji with a known smile on his face said- Boys, a seed that held the "potential for greatness". The seed, when planted in fertile soil and nurtured with care, could grow into a mighty tree that provided share, shelter, and sustenance. As you see we are sitting under such a tree (it was a Neem Tree), which might have been planted by our grandfather "He continued to explain about goal setting. He said that goal setting is much like planting a seed. At this point, as a curious boy, Ramdas asked, "Guru Ji, what is this seed holding within?" As there was no clear answer for him, Guru Ji appreciated Ramdas's inquisitiveness and said:" The seed represents an idea, a dream, or an aspiration. But the seed needs the right conditions to sprout and grow. Similarly, our goals require careful planning, dedication, and a nurturing environment. The environment of respect, trust, love, and mutual understanding.

Guru Ji continued further illustrating the foundational principles of goal setting: Clear objectives, creating a detailed plan, adapting to challenges, and perseverance with determination were his words for the team.

The team understood the power of goal setting and achieving goals. That year the Holi celebration was the best!! I still remember that colorful day with sweets and happiness all around.

In this episode of our journey, we will discuss the following.

1. Foundation of Goal Setting: Importance of Goal Setting

2. Strategic Planning for Success: Making actionable plans to achieve objectives.

3. SMART Goal Framework: Exploring the SMART criteria (Specific, Measurable, Achievable, Relevant, Time-Bound) and applying SMART principles to personal and team goals.

4. Aligning Individual and Team Goals: Encouraging collaboration in goal-setting.

5. Adopting Goals to Changing Environment: Navigating challenges and uncertainties in goal setting.

6. Leadership's Role in Goal Attainment: How leaders can influence goal-setting processes!

7. Effective Communication for Goal Achievement: Encouraging open dialogues within a team.

8. Measuring and Celebrating Success: Establishing key performance indicators. Recognizing and celebrating individual and collective achievements.

9. Learning from Failure: Embracing failure as a part of the goal-setting journey. Key lessons learned

10. Sustaining motivation: Maintaining enthusiasm to sustain long-term motivation.

The Foundation of Effective Goal Setting-

IMPORTANCE OF GOAL SETTING

"A year from now you may wish you had started today."

- Karen Lamb

In the vast landscape of personal and professional development, one principle stands as the solid foundation of success: effective goal setting. Goals provide us with direction, purpose, and a roadmap for progress. Goals, in our life, act as the guiding star in the constellation of our aspirations, leading us to fulfill our dreams and aspirations.

Vision: At the heart of effective goal setting lies the power of vision. Imagine you have to cross a dense forest and don't have a clear direction but you are eager to embark on a journey. Can you take a call to start the journey without a clear direction? In the same way, you are on a journey of professional success. And without a clear direction, the journey is an overwhelming expanse of uncertainty. Goal transforms the ambiguity of the unknown or uncertainty into a purposeful and structured journey. Goals give us vision, a focal point towards which we can channel our energy, efforts, And enthusiasm.

Objectives: To build a solid foundation for effective goal setting, you must craft clear and measurable objectives. Usually, people are stuck here because they are not able to differentiate between Goals and desires. Desires are unlimited. Goals should never be unlimited, Goals should be specific, so there is no room for ambiguity. You must know what you aim to achieve. Then only you can pave the way for a focused and intentional approach. Measurable means, providing a yardstick for progress, so you track your journey.

STORYTIME

In my village, we had a very skilled carpenter who was very famous for designing any difficult structure. One day the school headmaster asked him to design the structure for the new building of the school. The Inspector of the school was scheduled to visit the village exactly after 10 days. Since the reputation of the carpenter was such the master did not ask many questions and assigned the task asking him to finish the structure with the color scheme by the next week. We noticed a peculiar thing, the carpenter was doing his job diligently but without having a clear plan and design. He was just making a structure with no proper measurement or color combination.

Luckily one day the headmaster of my school asked him to show the structure and to his biggest surprise he noticed the structure did not have even proper alignment and color combination was so poor that looked very odd. With anger on his face, my school headmaster asked him, "Why did you build this structure without a clear plan? It lacks the quality and functionality I expected." The carpenter realized his mistake and responded" I am sorry Sir, I failed to set a clear goal for this project. I worked without a vision and as a result, the structure lacks the excellence I am capable of creating." He was under the impression that the headmaster was asking this structure to see his capabilities and did not realize the inspection of the school structure. Since Carpenter was highly skilled he could finish the structure in time and the building was approved and we had a new school building in my village.

EXERCISE

Please list your key Learnings:

1.

2.

3.

4.

The ancient wisdom reminds us that, in both personal and professional pursuits, it is important to have a clear goal. A clear goal is like a compass that guides us for meaningful and impactful actions.

This will ensure that our efforts are aligned with a purposeful outcome.

Let me share another real-time story. As tory of perfect planning and execution of plan.

Here is the story of a former colleague of mine, Mahendra, who worked at the same organization as me. He was an aspiring runner with a dream to complete a marathon. We all encouraged him to not only finish the race but to do so within a specific timeframe. Mahendra began to believe in himself, envisioning crossing the finish line with a surge of accomplishment. This vision served as the driving force behind his training sessions, early morning runs, and sacrifices.

Mahendra set a clear goal for himself: to complete a marathon within six months. Each week, he set measurable objectives to increase his running distance, improve his pace, and monitor his stamina. His journey was not easy, as he faced challenges such as sore muscles, doubts, and the temptation to give up. However, Mahendra's commitment to himself propelled him forward.

On the day of the marathon, Mahendra stood at the starting line with a pounding heart, anticipating the moment when he would finally cross the finish line. He visualized himself standing at the finish line, mentally preparing himself to be a winner. What was once a distant vision was now within his reach. He crossed the distance and made it to the finish line, fulfilling his dream through effective goal-setting.

Mahendra's story teaches us that a well-defined goal, coupled with determination and a never-give-up attitude, can turn into something tangible. The foundation of effective goal setting rests on the pillars of vision, clarity, and measurability. As we start our journey of exploration and growth, let us embrace the profound impact that purposeful goal-setting can have on our lives. Each one of us has the transformative potential that Mahendra had in him. So let us start preparing for a journey of aspirations and happiness.

STRATEGIC PLANNING FOR SUCCESS

Making Actionable Plans To Achieve Objectives:

"Success is 20% skills and 80% strategies. You must know how to succeed, but more importantly, what's your plan to succeed."

- Jim Rohn

Strategic planning is a systematic and comprehensive process that you should undertake to define your long-term goals and Objectives. This can be your personal goals as an individual or at the organizational level as a leader. Goals have no meaning without a plan. So you need to develop a plan of action to achieve your Goals.

Strategic planning involves the following steps...

Analyzing the current state of affairs- Do a SWOT analysis; Strengths, Weaknesses, Opportunities, and Threats.

Setting Priorities

Making decisions on allocating resources

Charting a course for the future- breaking down strategies into actionable steps- task/responsibilities/timeline and resources required to implement the chosen strategy.

Monitoring progress- This involves monitoring KPI (Key Performance Indicators) and comparing actual performance with the planned benchmarks. By doing so, you can identify successes, areas for improvement, and the need for adjustments to the strategic plan.

Since strategic planning is an ongoing process it requires feedback, flexibility, and adaptability. You can achieve success by aligning actions with a clear vision and purpose. Remember, "Action without purpose is a waste of time" Activity is more than action, it is

"Action = Activity +Purpose"

Why is strategic planning crucial in the pursuit of goals?

Strategic planning plays a pivotal role in goal achievement. It acts as the compass that guides you and your organization toward success.

There are many reasons why strategic planning is important in the pursuit of goals.

1. It provides a clear sense of direction. You can align your actions and the efforts of your team members toward a common goal. You can minimize distractions and hence can improve efficiency.

2. It will help in evaluating resources and capabilities. This means if you can allocate resources effectively, you can maximize their impact. This means efforts are in the right direction and on those activities which are purposeful. There will be prevention of resource wastage on non-essential activities.

3. It will equip you with the ability to anticipate and respond to changes, challenges, and opportunities. It will keep you focused on the ultimate goal.

4. Setting specific and challenging goals through strategic planning can serve as a powerful motivator. if you can articulate purpose clearly to the team, then you can inspire a shared sense of purpose among all team members.

5. You can allocate resources as per the criticality of tasks. Such prioritization ensures that efforts are concentrated on high-impact activity. This means you can improve the efficiency and effectiveness of team members.

6. SWOT analysis will help you in identifying potential risks and challenges. This proactive approach will always help you develop a plan B in times of crisis and will reduce the impact of any obstacles that may come as a surprise.

7. There is the benefit of strategic planning in Organizational learning. You can gain valuable insights, if you can analyze past experiences, successes, and failures, to continuous learning and development.

So we can say that strategic planning serves as a compass that not only points individuals and organizations in the right direction but also equips them with the right tools and insights needed to navigate the complexities.

The main advantage of strategic planning is its ability to translate aspirations into actionable plans.

SMART GOAL FRAMEWORK

Applying SMART principles to personal and team goals.

"If you want to be happy, set a goal that commands your thoughts, liberates your energy, and inspires your hopes."

- Andrew Carnegie

S- Specific

M- Measurable

A- Achievable

R- Relevant

T- Time-bound

I know one of the salespeople who was working for LIC as an Insurance agent and later he became a development officer with Life Insurance Corporation Ltd (LIC).

I met him long back and I was so impressed with his approach that he was the person who managed all my insurance policies for my family and friend circle. His approach was very simple and he was very methodical. I am happy to share my learnings and the approach that made him so successful.

Meet Ramdas, a determined insurance salesman with a vision to become the top performer in his agency. I understood from Ramdas that he was very clear that success in the competitive world of insurance sales required more than just ambition. The need was to have a strategic approach. He understood the power of SMART goals and made an integral part of his journey.

Specific- Ramdas used to share with me that his initial goal was to enhance his sales performance, but he knew specificity was key. He had a general target- "I want to improve my sales performance".

Ramdas set a specific goal: to increase his monthly sales by 10%. He said this 10% increase brought clear focus and defined direction for his efforts.

Measurable- Ramdas shared one of his encounters he had with his manager, he said," If you can't measure your progress then it is very difficult to make any progress". after that, I started tracking my daily calls, and meetings with my prospects who were my future customers, said Ramdas.

He said this simple sales log helped him a lot to quantify his performance against the 10% increase target. This tracking kept him motivated throughout.

Achievable- A very interesting thing Ramdas shared during one of my meetings with him, he said, "In the beginning, I was frustrated as I planned 20% Increase as my Goal". then Ramdas continued to explain, the goal must be achievable but ambitious and still realistic. I asked him to share more about this. He said, I learned from my Manager, that overly ambitious goals could lead to frustration and burnout. Instead, he suggested to asses my client base, market trends, and my capabilities. With this realistic perspective, Ramdas set achievable sub-goals, such as expanding my client base network and refining my pitch. This approach ensured a steady progress towards the ultimate objective.

Relevant- Ramdas shared that his goal was deeply relevant to his career aspirations and the demands of the insurance sector. Achieving a 10% increase in monthly sales wasn't just about numbers- it was about establishing himself as a reliable and trustworthy professional in the industry.

Time-Bound- this always helps to instill a sense of urgency. Ramdas set a timeframe for his goal. The 10% increase was to be accomplished within the next quarter. He said, this time-bound approach created a sense of accountability and pushed him to implement his strategies promptly.

As a curious person, I always used to ask Ramdas about his progress, and in one such interaction, I asked him did he ever faced any challenges in achieving his goal. Any rejections from his potential clients? And how did he manage these situations? He shared many examples and said with confidence of his face. "I implemented my SMART goal, challenges emerged- rejections from potential clients, market fluctuations, and unforeseen objections, yet, armed with the SMART framework, I adapted my approach, refined my sales techniques, and consistently moved towards my target."

I requested Ramdas during one of our get-togethers with common friends to share a few challenges and his approach that has helped him to overcome challenges. Ramdas was quite excited to share his experiences and I feel this will help you to be a better salesperson in your life. Here are a few examples shared by Ramdas.

Challenges faced by Ramdas as he shared were as follows:

1- Budget constraints- that was the # 1 challenge faced by him.

2- Lack of Decision-Maker Engagement – this was another challenge faced by him.

3- We are Currently Satisfied with our Insurance Provider- Many prospects were hesitant to switch from their current provider.

4- I don't have time – this was another common challenge faced by him.

Effective approaches of Ramdas in his own words:

A- Active Listening- most salespersons fail here as they are in a hurry and don't spend time.

B- Ask open-ended questions- (open-ended questions are those questions that can not be answered in simple Yes, or No but need more clarification). This approach allows you to tailor your response more effectively. For example: What are your top priorities when it comes to insurance coverage?

C- Provide information that addresses the prospect's concern and they get clarity on how your product or service can specifically meet their needs.

D- Handle Rejections Positively- every rejection allows you to learn more.

E- Relationship Building- the biggest investment in any relationship is time and don't focus on immediate sales but on future opportunities.

Ramdas shared, that each individual has unique challenges and goals, so you need to be specific to his needs. Once you are spending time with your prospects with a genuine approach then it is easy to identify their specific needs. One thing Ramdas was practicing, as shared by him; sharing success stories, from his satisfied customers. This helped him build credibility and address doubts about his prospects.

I asked him a specific question, have you ever faced price objections? His approach is worth appreciating. he said, price is never a challenge but an opportunity. Focus on the value and benefits of your offering and not on price negotiation. Ramdas said I was focusing on my prospects about how his investment aligns with his long-term goals. This was unique to each prospect and decision making was easy to them. By practicing this approach, Ramdas became a trusted advisor to his clients and future deals became easy. He was getting regular referrals and he revised his goals upward to increase his target by 5% for every month's sales.

Ramdas summarized; that by understanding and proactively addressing these challenges and objections, I enhanced my effectiveness and could build stronger, long-lasting relationships with prospects and clients.

Let us revisit our learnings.

Here are two examples, write against each example which is following SMART criteria and which one is not.

Goal A- I will increase my marketing efforts to achieve my growth target.

Goal B- I will increase my sales revenue by 15% in the next quarter through targeted marketing campaigns.

Explanation:

Goal A – Non SMART Goal

Reasons It's not SMART:

Not Specific- There is no clarity on which aspect of marketing needs improvement.

Not Measurable- There is no quantifiable metric to gauge improvement.'

Not Achievable- It is vague, making it challenging to determine what success looks like.

Not Relevant- Doesn't specify how improved marketing ties to broader objectives.

Not Time-Bound- Doesn't have a time frame for achieving improvement.

Goal B- SMART Criteria

Why is it SMART

Specific- Increase sales revenue by 15%

Measurable: the percentage increase provides a clear measure of success.

Achievable- the Goal is realistic and attainable.

Relevant- Aligned with the business objective of revenue growth.

Time-Bound- Achieve the increase within the next three months.

EXERCISE: NO 1

Please select one personal goal you want to achieve: it could be related to your Health and wellness, Personal development, or any other area that find meaningful.

Make a SMART plan if you have a dream to have 3 Bed Room House.

Specific-

Measurable-

Achievable-

Realistic-

Time-Bound-

Keep a few challenges like; property rate may go up and you may have some financial emergencies to keep in mind while doing exercise.

Have clear Strategies for success – diversify savings with a mix of short–term and long-term investment options. Revisit your saving plans based on market trends.

EXERCISE: NO 2

Professional Goal- ex; Getting promoted to the next level

Select SMART Criteria-

Specific:

Measurable:

Achievable:

Relevant:

Time-bound:

You need to bear potential challenges in mind – it may be competing with colleagues for advancement opportunities. Balancing increased responsibilities with existing workload.

Design your Strategies for success-

Setting a SMART goal for career advancement provides a structured approach. What will help you?

Regular feedback and effective communication from your leader will help you.

Proactive skill development will help you (you may require new skills to be successful in the next role).

Your leader will contribute a lot to achieving the goal of securing a promotion within a specified time frame so seek his support and guidance.

My suggestion: "Ensure a clear and actionable plan".

Set goals that are both attainable (Achievable) and ambitious. You need to keep a balance that can significantly impact you as an individual or your organization's success. Never be overambitious.

Why Not Over ambitious? There is the risk of burnout. It can shake your confidence. You may lose interest which may lead to disengagement.

Why attainable and ambitious?

This balances the risk-taking ability of an individual. Attainable goals are realistic goals that provide a foundation for risk-taking. You can have manageable boundaries.

Ambitious goals involve calculated risks on a larger scale.

Why attainable/achievable?

These goals are within reach. they will provide a sense of accomplishment once you complete it. This will keep your motivation high and will encourage continued efforts.

Realistic/relevant- setting realistic goals helps avoid unnecessary frustration. It reinforces the belief that one can overcome challenges and succeed in the future. Regular achievements create a positive momentum.

EXERCISE

Set your professional goal for your next promotion.

Follow SMART Criteria, keeping it attainable and yet ambitious.

"The trouble with not having a goal is that you can spend your life running up and down the field and never score."

- *Bill Copeland (an American poet and historian)*

ALIGNING INDIVIDUAL AND TEAM GOALS

ENCOURAGING COLLABORATION IN GOAL-SETTING

"The People who are crazy enough to think they can change the world are the ones who do."

- Steve Jobs

What are individual goals in the organization? This is an important question. I have seen many managers talking about the alignment of individual goals with organizational goals. But the question remains about what is the difference between individual and organizational goals, and how to align these goals.

Individual goals focus on factors that are key results, outcomes, and/ or deliverables. Employee works to achieve organizational goals. To achieve larger goals, employees need to build skills or enhance their knowledge.

Organizational goals cover all aspects of employees, work, and products.

Why align individual goals with organizational goals? You will agree that no organization can achieve its goals if employees are not aligned with the same cause. They need to match the larger goals of the organization.

Strong teamwork will lead to optimum performance, there will be a sense of belonging and personal satisfaction. The organizations where there is a culture of cohesion, they don't suffer from the problem of attrition. People want to stay with the organization. People are actively engaged in the organization.

As a leader, you must focus on how your team members interact with each other. How is the atmosphere? Is this conducive to reaching the organization's goals? Employee engagement means the level of their commitment. An individual contributes willingly to the growth of the organization. There are many research papers available today that prove that collaborative problem-solving leads to better outcomes. They support each other, they encourage each other to take calculated risks that lead to innovation. They take the risk because they know, they have the support of a team behind them. Remember- Innovation is not discovery but to do the same thing in a better way that exists.

Team building activities- leaders who are progressive and promote teamwork, always involve their team members in such activities. They know team-building activities will create an environment of trust, friendship, and understanding.

I remember my team leader was always organizing fun bonding activities during regular cycle meetings and annual budget meetings. Fun bonding activities like scavenger hunts or karaoke nights were very common. We were having problem-solving tasks as well. These activities can help build relationships between team members. The advantage of such activities is always more productive work and a happier team.

In the words of Henry Ford- *"Coming together is a beginning staying together is progress and working together is success."*

I remember one of such scavenger hunt activities we carried out in the state of Kerala, we had a language barrier. We were given a clue and with that clue we had to identify the place and reach there to get the next clue and so on. Our first clue was- Rose Flower, 2nd clue was a big international event. Our team could identify the place with these 2 clues only. It was Jawahar Lal Nehru Cricket Stadium. The next clue was a photograph of a building and naturally team needed a local person who could help us to identify that building and we felt the importance of language. There were a few more such clues and our team was the winning team. I am sharing the strategies that helped us-

1- Communication and Transparency: we had open communication about team goals and individual contributions. Everyone has to contribute it be as simple as keeping track of time or spending during the journey etc. Everyone understood how their work contributes to overall team success.

2- Clarify Team Objectives: today I can say with a sense of satisfaction that my team leader clearly defined and articulated team objectives so well that even today I remember them word by word.

When team members have a shared understanding of the collective goals, they can align their individual goals to support the team's mission.

There are more suggestions that I received from my seniors. There is power in those suggestions and I am sharing a few with you here.

3- Individual Goal-Setting Sessions: I was advised to conduct individual goal-setting sessions. The idea was to understand each team member's aspirations. Each individual is unique so are their aspirations. They must set their goals as per their aspiration and not as per your simple advice. I suggest listing areas of improvement for each team member as well. So they know their strengths and areas where they have to work to be better professionals tomorrow. Now the real task or priority is to align individual goals with overarching team objectives. The benefits that I have experienced in my life were beyond my imagination.

4- The impact of their action was huge. They had a sense of satisfaction. They were contributing willingly. There was a sense of accountability for their actions. There was a celebration. There was open feedback and criticism without hurting the feelings of others.

5- Everyone felt like a winner, a real hero, they were engaged with a large purpose and the feeling of

6- one team one goal always kept them going in the same direction.

As a leader, it is your prime responsibility to set clear organizational goals.

Remember- Value flows from top to bottom and never the other way around.

So Goal alignment has to start with you. what is the vision of the company, what is your core strategy and share specific goals you want to achieve as a team? My leaders communicated in one such session; "we want to be the largest and fastest growing team within the organization". if you read it again it will sound like a target that is crystal clear to everyone. Isn't it?

Benefits of having clear goals- The clearer the goals, the easier understanding by team members.

Remember- General goals will lead to general results.

What should be the strategy then?

I would like to share my experience with you. My former leader had a great leadership style which involved taking his core team members into confidence. He shared the company's vision and strategy with us and encouraged us to give feedback and suggestions. He was very open to listening to our opinions, and we were free to ask any questions to get a better understanding of the goals. Once everyone on the core team was on board, the execution of the strategy became much smoother. Adopting this leadership style has many benefits, including clear communication of goals at every level of the organization..

Remember- ensure, strategic, clear, and consistent communication with the team.

I suggest- Make goals a regular part of your meetings.

My leader was a firm believer in helping the team to achieve their goals. He always used to say- you can't succeed in a vacuum. Everyone needs support to set and achieve goals.

EXERCISE

Please write a few points on support required by an employee if-

1. He is a new hire.

2. He is an Existing employee.

Remember: Review the progress to ensure work is on track. Provide resources and tools to effectively get the job done.

> "I can't change the direction of the wind, but I can adjust my sails to always reach my destination."
>
> *- Jimmy Dean*

1- **Collaboration:** My leader was always promoting a collaborative culture. We were supporting each other in achieving our shared goals. Since we were sharing the expertise and resources that enhanced overall team performance, and we were a winning team almost every time.

2- Recognition and Reward: I learned to recognize and reward both individual and team achievements. The magic of this reward and recognition was contributing to the success of the entire team. Each individual's success contributed to the success of the team.

3- Adaptability and Flexibility: this is a challenge and opportunity as well. You have to recognize that individual goals may need to adapt based on shifting team priorities. You as a leader have to play a big role in fostering a culture that values flexibility and encourages individuals to pivot when necessary for the team.

4- Performance Metrics: you have to create a natural connection between individual efforts and overall team success. Design individual performance metrics are aligned with the team KPI (Key Performance Indicators)

Let me share a few examples of my life so that you get more clarity on Individual Goals and team goals'

I have 4 Zonal Leaders and each Zonal Manager has a specific target for monthly sales revenue. They were supposed to achieve their numbers and this was their individual goal.

Team Goal; We always had an aim to achieve a certain percentage increase in market share compared to the previous quarter.

Each individual was achieving his target and they were contributing to the overall sales targets. But as a team, we had different goals which were common or shared so we were getting breakthrough ideas and new strategies to beat the market growth and do better than nearest competitors. Collectively they were doing better and we were exceeding the team goal.

EXERCISE

You have a project to complete in the next 30 days.

What can be an Individual goal?

What is the team goal?

How will you align individual and team goals?

KEY CONSIDERATIONS

I suggest considering the following to be an effective team leader in aligning individual and team goals;

1- Establish a shared vision and set of values that resonate with both individual and team goals. Benefit- when everyone is working towards a common purpose, alignment becomes more natural.

2- Consider how individual goals align with the professional growth and development of team members. Benefit- team members will develop their skill set and will also acquire new skills that will benefit both individuals and the team.

3- Adopt a goal cascade approach. Benefit- this will ensure seamless alignment from top to bottom.

4- Implement regular feedback mechanisms. Benefit- this input will give a clear idea to the individual on how his contribution impacts the team dynamics. This will also help to refine the alignment process.

5- Monitor the Progress- this is essential. Benefit- this will help you in making adjustments as needed.

6- Foster an environment where team members actively support each other in achieving their goals. Benefit- this will reinforce the interdependence of individual and team success.

These strategies and considerations will help align individual and team goals, driving collective success and fostering shared achievement.

ADOPTING GOALS TO CHANGING ENVIRONMENT

NAVIGATING CHALLENGES AND UNCERTAINTIES IN GOAL SETTING

"The strongest will in the will that knows how to bend."

- Alice Duer Miller

Adapting goals to an evolving environment becomes a vital skill. The good news is that we can learn this skill. In this chapter, we will explore the art of goal adaptation. With my experience, will try to provide insights into navigating challenges and fostering resilience.

Let us understand factors that can impact goals.

External factors- it is very important to monitor the external factors that impact goals, for example- Market trends, new technology, socioeconomic changes on so on.

There are tools available to use and understand the external factors and their impact.

If you are working in an environmentally sensitive industry or export-oriented units then I would suggest, **PESTLE Analysis.**

PESTLE ANALYSIS

You can use this analysis to evaluate external factors systematically-

Political- Assess the Influence of Government Policies, stability of Government, and potential changes on your goals.

Economic- evaluate the impact of economic conditions, such as inflation, exchange rates, and market trends, on your goals.

Social- Consumer behavior, cultural trends, or demographics may affect your goals.

Technological- Analyze the role of technology, innovation, and digital advancement in shaping and impacting your goals.

Legal – consider the legal environment, including regulations, compliance requirements, and potential legal challenges to your goals.

Environmental – Explore how ecological and climate-related considerations might affect your goals.

If you are working in sales, have an interest in business, or product management, or working on a project, then use SWOT Analysis;

SWOT ANALYSIS

This analysis helps us to assess both internal factors impacting your goals.

Strengths/Weaknesses/Opportunities/ Threats

SWOT analysis is a versatile tool and can be used across industries. It provides a structured framework for evaluating internal Strengths and Weaknesses and external opportunities and threats.

Let me share a few examples to make it clearer.

You are working on product development: in that case, SWOT Analysis can assist you in understanding market demands, internal capabilities, and potential challenges, ensuring a more informed product development strategy.

In the case of Marketing Planning- SWOT analysis is valuable for assessing a company's positioning in the market, understanding customer perceptions, and identifying opportunities for growth or areas of improvement.

In case you are working in the Human resources department of an Organization, then SWOT analysis can be applied to assess the strengths and weaknesses of the workforce, identify the opportunity for skill development, and recognize potential threats to employee satisfaction. And let me share one more example.

Personal Development: you can use SWOT analysis for personal development planning. it will help you identify your strengths, weaknesses, opportunities for growth, and potential threats to personal success.

EXERCISE

Take personal development as one area to use SWOT analysis.

Strength- Identify your key strengths, skills, and talents. You may consider, education, experience, and your personal qualities.

Weaknesses- Reflect on areas where you feel less confident or lack certain skills.

Opportunities- explore external opportunities that align with your goals, and consider trends, networking opportunities, education, or personal development programs.

Threats- identify external factors that may pose challenges to your personal development. Consider economic conditions, industry trends, or personal challenges.

Make Action Plan: mention the steps you need to take to achieve your personal development goals. Keep timelines, resources needed, and milestones for tracking the progress in mind.

By applying SWOT analysis to personal development, you create a strategic roadmap that aligns your strengths with opportunities, addresses weaknesses, and prepares you to face potential challenges. Use the tool effectively in your personal growth.

MARKET TRENDS

You must be well informed about current market trends that could affect your industry or field in which you are working. Get reports, attend conferences, and be in touch with industry experts to anticipate shifts and adjust goals accordingly.

COMPETITIVE LANDSCAPE

You need to be aware of your competitor's activities and strategies. You should study their success and failure to get real useful insights into adapting your goals to stay competitive.

Case study: "Netflix", As you know in the early 2000s, Netflix primarily operated as a DVD rental-by-mail service, revolutionizing the home entertainment industry. Over time there were more options like digital streaming and there was a change in consumer preferences. And company faced a significant challenge to its existing business model.

Challenge: the biggest challenge to the company was to remain competitive. The shift in consumer behaviour was towards online streaming and there was a threat to Netflix's DVD rental model.

Adapting Goals: Strategic Shift- Netflix embraced a strategic shift from DVD to online streaming. This was a shift from its primary goal of being a DVD rental service to becoming a leading streaming platform.

Content Creation- If you want to remain competitive then you need to be ahead of your competitors. Netflix knew this well and invested heavily in original content production. They set a goal to create compelling, exclusive shows and movies.

Global Reach: Realizing the global potential of streaming, Netflix set a goal to expand its services internationally, tapping into diverse markets to cater to diverse cultures and languages.

Execution: Netflix's global audience was attracted by shows like "House of Cards", "Stranger Things", and "The Crown", which proved to be the key to its success.

Results: Netflix became a leading market player after a strategic shift that resulted in a global surge of subscribers. Today, millions of people consider Netflix as their primary source of entertainment.

KEY LEARNINGS

Netflix's success demonstrates the importance of **agile goal setting**.

Netflix focused on the preferences of consumers and not on the products they had.

Netflix made innovation a core goal and as a result, they stayed ahead of the competition.

My Take: The journey of Netflix is a prime example of how adapting your goals in the face of challenges can be transformative. They continuously set new objectives that align with market trends and manage challenges effectively, using them as opportunities. As a result, they have become a leader in their industry today.

Adaptability, a few examples from great Business houses in India.: "If I had to give an example of adaptability in business, the name Reliance Industries and its chairman Mukesh Ambani come to mind. They have shown exceptional adaptability in navigating the company through various business landscapes. Initially a textile manufacturing company, in the 1980s when the industry faced challenges, they shifted their focus to petrochemicals, and today, they are the industry leader. Another remarkable story of their adaptability is Reliance Jio, which has disrupted the industry with affordable data and transformed the way Indians use the internet."

The success stories of Ratan Tata and the Tata Group are significant examples that demonstrate the importance of adaptability. Thanks to Ratan Tata's leadership and adaptability, the Tata Group became a global powerhouse with a presence in diverse industries. In 1991, Ratan Tata became the chairman of Tata Sons during a time of economic uncertainty and global competition. These examples highlight how adaptability, innovation, and commitment to core values can drive success, even in the face of adversity and uncertainty.

Storytime: if you are in sales, then you can resonate with this ancient story that is a good example of Adaptability and clever problem-solving.

One day, Mulla Naseruddin as frantically searching for his lost keys under a streetlight. A neighbor passing by asked," Mulla, are you sure lost your key here?" Mulla Naseruddin replied," No, I lost it in my house, but it's too dark inside. I can't see anything. So, I am looking for the keys here where there's more light."

The neighbor, puzzled, said, "But Mulla, if you have lost the keys inside your house, why are you searching for it outside?"

Mulla Naseruddin, with a mischievous smile, responded," Well, the light is much better here, Isn't it?"

Moral of the story: Mulla Naseruddin's humorous approach highlights the importance of adapting strategies to the situation at hand.

Sometimes, the solution requires a shift in perspective and willingness to adapt to new circumstances.

Remember- "Be ready to adapt new strategies as per the situation" and, 'always think out of the box'.

True Value of Resilience in achieving your goals:

Resilience is not just about recovering from adversity. Rather, it is the skill of emerging from challenges stronger, wiser, and more determined than before. Its true value lies in its ability to help us navigate the unpredictable twists and turns that come with pursuing our goals. When unexpected challenges arise, resilience becomes our compass, guiding us back on course with unwavering resolve.

SUCCESS STORY & THE TRUE POWER OF RESILIENCE

I have shared the inspiring story of Soichiro Honda in my books, and I would like to share a short story about his resilience with you. As you may know, Soichiro Honda came to the city from his small village with big dreams. However, his first setback came when his innovative piston ring design was rejected by Toyota. Rather than giving up, Honda used this defeat as an opportunity to improve his skills. This rejection catalyzed his relentless pursuit of excellence.

STORYTIME

During World War II, Honda's factories were reduced to rubble, posing unprecedented challenges. Despite the devastation, Honda saw potential in the ruins and leveraged his resilience by pivoting to producing motorized bicycles. He demonstrated a remarkable ability to adapt and innovate amidst adversity, leading to the launch of the Honda Dream. The Dream was not just a motorcycle, but it was also the embodiment of Honda's triumph over setbacks. The roar of the engine echoed through the corridors of automotive history, marking the rebirth of the company and the realization of Honda's enduring dream.

Each hardship and rejection fuelled Honda's determination, pushing him towards his audacious goals. The saga of Soichiro Honda exemplifies the transformative power of resilience.

Let us learn and Remember- "In the realm of goal-setting, resilience is not just a virtue; it is the engine that propels us forward."

Jack Welch once said, "Change before you have to"

So far,

We have understood the Foundation of Goal Setting and the importance of goal setting. Strategic planning for success- Strategic approach to goal setting

SMART Goal Framework- exploring the SMART Criteria with examples- Specific/ Measurable/Attainable/Achievable, Relevant/Realistic, and Time-Bound. Aligning Individual and Team Goals- establishing coherence between personal and team goals. The power of collaboration in goal setting.

Adapting goals to changing environment- with examples of Mukesh Ambani and Ratan Tata.

Now let us move forward and together we will understand the role of a leader in goal achievement.

LEADERSHIP'S ROLE IN GOAL ATTAINMENT

HOW LEADERS CAN INFLUENCE GOAL-SETTING PROCESSES

"A leader is one who knows the way, goes the way, and shows the way."

- John C, Maxwell

Effective leadership is essential to achieve organizational goals. Sometimes data may be misleading, or not give the full picture of the situation, and in such a situation, there is the role of the leadership team. As said by Gen. Collin Powell, *"Great leaders are almost always great simplifiers who can cut through argument, debate, and doubt to offer a solution everybody can understand."*

It reminds me of one of the brainstorming sessions to launch a combination of two drugs to manage acid peptic disorders. Data were not in favor of the choice of molecules that we were looking at and the Business Development team was not in favor of our choice and were insisting on choosing another choice which was there. We as a team had a dream to make our business a leading force in the area of acid peptic disorder. Our leader has been very effective in his role and has proved his understanding of the market to management so he had having support of senior management and his team was a strong team full of commitment and passion to deliver the results. There are people in every society who are always there to create hurdles, misuse their power, and try to influence the atmosphere, so my organization was not an exception as well. But leadership was strong enough to overrule the power of one such influencer in the Organization.

My leader convinced the senior leadership team and got their nod to go ahead with our choice of molecule. The mother brand was also de growing and the turnover of the mother brand was 50 Crore at that time and successful launch of a line extension with a combination and new indication, the brand created a sensation within the organization. The line extension achieved a landmark figure of 100 Crore and as a result of the efforts of the team the mother brand too crossed the 100 Cr figure and was growing at a very healthy double-digit growth.

We used to discuss and debate those moments, if my leader had accepted what was there in the data, then the company might have missed the 200 Cr opportunity (at that time and we can count still....) So the role of an effective leader is to provide direction, set clear direction, and clear expectations for their team to follow.

A leader with a vision for his organization's goal can set the tone for the team performance by inspiring and by creating a conducive work environment. We had such an inspirational leader who was always promoting collaboration among us. I have shared one beautiful and worthwhile experience that was shared by one of my team members in my book, he said, "I never thought that my workplace could be a second home for me". What else can you expect from your leader?

I have shared the qualities of a leader in my book ***"Mastering the Art of Rising Together"*** in detail.

One day during one of the manager's development programs the facilitator gave us a wonderful opportunity to learn and make an action plan for ourselves. He masked the therapy areas and brand, but gave a case study and asked participants to identify the characteristics every leader should have!

EXERCISE

Use this case study and list your points-

1.

2.

3.

4.

5.

Let me share my understanding and you can add more from your analysis and understanding.

He was under pressure to make his decision against the advice of the business development team.

Was this leader decisive?

Was he enjoying trust among his team? Can you build trust overnight? No, you can't build trust overnight. Building trust takes time and consistent effort. I suggest to follow the following to cultivate trustworthiness:

Consistency- your team will observe your behavior to see you are predictable and you are reliable.

Honesty and transparency- be open and honest in your communication.

Integrity- when you have strong principles and you follow them in life.

Competence- develop professional competence and expertise in your field. Acquire new knowledge and skills that will build confidence in your ability to lead effectively.

Empathy- your genuine interest in people's well-being. This will also help you to build trust.

Delegate and trust- trust your team members with responsibilities and empower them to make decisions.

My suggestion to my young leaders was: "Respect confidentiality and handle sensitive information with utmost care".

Remember- "Building trust is an ongoing process, and it requires continuous attention to these principles".

In one of my books, I have shared one experience of one of my old pharma colleagues, who used manager for one & leader to another of his senior to whom he had reported. I feel it is important to share their roles (manager and leader), and impact on a team's success.

The manager's role is about- Planning, organizing, and controlling processes.

The Leader's role is about- igniting inspiration and fostering a shared vision.

This means you have to play both the roles, the role of a manager and the role of a leader. You should be clear when to play which role and that is the secret of the success of effective leadership.

If you have a short focus on executing tasks and short-term goals, then you need to be in the role of a manager, and when you need to provide a compelling vision that extends beyond the day-to-day operations, then you have play the role of a leader.

Leadership is about connecting individual roles to a broader purpose. Leaders take pain in explaining why the work matters, inspiring team members by demonstrating how their contributions can make a world of difference in achieving collective success.

Leaders always lead from the front. They practice the values and work ethics they expect from their team. They create a model of excellence. This behavior builds trust and credibility. You will agree that these are the essential components of effective leadership.

Let me take a moment and summarize it.

Leadership is the force that propels a team beyond routine tasks toward a collective vision.

Management is essential for day-to-day operations. Leadership provides the inspiration, guidance, and emotional intelligence needed to transform a group of individuals into a cohesive and motivated team pursuing shared objectives. Effective leadership is all about getting the best out of each individual's contribution to achieve greater heights and a brighter future for the team.

STORYTIME

You may have heard stories about Akbar and Birbal. Here's one that can add value to our discussion and with which you can easily relate.

Let me say a few words;

About Birbal: the witty and wise advisor in the royal court of Emperor Akbar. Known for his sharp intellect and ingenious solutions. He is a symbol of wisdom and humor in the court. About Emperor Akbar: A visionary ruler known for his intelligence and love for challenges, in his court, Birbal, was more than an advisor but a trusted confidant to the mighty emperor.

Now enjoy reading-

One day, Akbar challenged Birbal to prove his leadership skills not by managing the affairs of the court but by inspiring the kingdom's subjects. Birbal accepted the challenge and came up with a plan. He gathered the kingdom's artisans, poets, and scholars and announced a grand competition. The participants were not supposed to create a masterpiece for the emperor but to collectively craft a symbol of unity and shared purpose. The artisans began sculpting, the poets penned verses, and the scholars contributed their knowledge and wisdom. Birbal didn't dictate the details but provided guidance and encouragement, creating an environment where each contributor felt a sense of ownership. As the project unfolded, the kingdom buzzed with creativity and collaboration. The unity among the diverse talents was palpable. Birbal didn't just manage the competition; he inspired a shared objective that transcended individual skills and roles. When the masterpiece was unveiled, it wasn't merely a work of art. It was a testament to the power of leadership. The symbol reflected the collective spirit of the kingdom, showcasing how different talents when guided by a unifying vision, could create something far greater than the sum of its parts.

The king, Akbar, was impressed by the outcome and asked Birbal about his approach. Birbal replied with a knowing smile," O Emperor, true leadership is not about commanding but about inspiring. By nurturing a shared purpose, we can turn ordinary tasks into extraordinary achievements.

MORAL OF THE STORY

Leadership, as exemplified by Birbal, is more than just managing a group of individuals. It is a journey of inspiring and collaborating with them. By weaving a narrative of purpose and unity, leaders can transform a group of individuals into a harmonious team that works together to achieve shared objectives.

Remember- "The art of leadership lies in fostering a shared vision that brings out the best in each contributor, creating a masterpiece that reflects the strength of unity."

EXERCISE

Imagine you are working as a leader in one of the large organizations. you have a challenge to bring robust performance by building a team.

Exercise the importance of leadership in fostering a shared vision and the transformative power of collaboration. What is the flow to engage your team in the creative process?

Here is a hint for you.

Start with an Objective:

Define a Shared Objective: It could be a project goal, a team motto, or a visual representation of your shared mission.

What lessons from Birbal's story can be applied to your exercise?

EFFECTIVE COMMUNICATION FOR GOAL ACHIEVEMENT

ENCOURAGING OPEN DIALOGUES WITHIN A TEAM

"Communication- the human connection is the key to personal and career success."

- Paul J Meyer

WHAT IS EFFECTIVE COMMUNICATION?

You will find many responses to this question and I would like to share my understanding.

Effective communication plays a pivotal role in the success journey of a leader.

"Communication is one of the most important skills you require for a successful life"

- Catherine Pulsifer

I developed my understanding of Effective Communication as; "when you exchange ideas, and thoughts with your team members and seek their opinion, and share data so that they understand the message with clarity. If they get the message with clarity and understand the purpose of your communication, is effective communication".

Effective communication can be humorous also and you can communicate very effectively without hurting the feelings of someone.

It reminds me of one episode that happened long back when we were new to emails and some of us used to struggle to share data. One of my Managers used to write very lengthy emails and was expecting a quick response from his team. The team was not very comfortable with his approach; Overall he was enjoying good relationships with his team and under his leadership team was a high-performing team. Some people approached me for my intervention. Initially, I was not willing to intervene in his operational style but when I started getting frequent requests, then I thought of communicating to save his relationships with his team. One day I suggested to one of his senior team members the following. It was an important matter that was on a priority list and everyone was involved and there was a timeline too but not that tight timeline. I suggested he delay the response for some time and wait for his reminder email or phone call. Once you get a reminder just write the following on the body of the email.

Sir, "I was taking a coffee break to complete reading your email as it was too long, I could not finish in one sitting."

This happened the same way and I am delighted to share that my manager took this as feedback and improved a lot. I could save their relationship and also could protect his self-esteem.

Remember: "Effective communication is not just about speaking but about listening, asking relevant and appropriate questions, and collaborating."

Let me share a story from my childhood and then we can discuss about key elements of effective communication.

STORYTIME

The Promise and the Box of Surprise

I was living in a village and it was rainy season. One day, a dear friend and my classmate arrived in my village to meet me. As he entered the lively park where children were playing and were enjoying their time. my friend decided to engage them on a quest to find my house.

Promising a reward to the kids who could guide him, a group of curious boys eagerly volunteered. He announced a reward as," I will give you something". Once they reached my house, they reminded my friend of his commitment and expected their reward, "Something"!. There was a small grocery shop near to my house. He took the children there and offered them chocolates, biscuits etc. My friend found the children insisting on something as promised by him. He was puzzled and very much confused about the reward, what to do,

Ramdas, witnessing the delightful commotion, stepped in with a twinkle in his eyes. He brought a small box covered by a cloth and handed it over to my friend, suggesting a creative way to fulfill the promise. The box contained a small frog, lively and jumping.

My friend with a shy of relief on his face, followed the suggestion of Ramdas, handed the box to the leader of the group, and asked them to be close to each other. My friend instructed them to announce what was inside the box before receiving their reward. The moment children got the box in their hand, they shouted in excitement saying, there is SOMETHING inside this box.

I learned a few lessons and I am happy to share them with you as key takeaways;

1- Effective communication involves being clear in promises and ensuring they are fulfilled.

2- Understand the audience's needs- Children were insisting on a specific reward. So it is important to understand and meet the needs and expectations of your audience. Otherwise, there is a possibility that you may end up paying more, and still, the audience is not satisfied.

3- Adaptation of communication style- Ramdas's creative solution demonstrates the significance of adapting communication style to capture the audience's attention and meet their expectations effectively.

4- Active engagement and Participation- in this story, we have seen the active participation of children, which showcases the concept of engaging your audience and involving them in communication.

5- Innovative Problem Solving—the introduction of a small frog as a surprise reveals the value of innovative problem-solving in communication. Unconventional approaches can lead to effective solutions. And very important-

6- Transparency and Announcing Expectations- there was transparency in communication, encouraging the audience (Children in this case) to announce their findings (There is something inside t this box) and creating a shared understanding.

Many such examples around us can teach us many lessons on, tailoring communication styles, the power of crafting compelling messages, and Navigating Difficult Conversations.

Let me share a story from one Indian Village: ***"The River of Milk: A Wedding Tale"***

STORYTIME

In the heart of a bustling village, preparations for a joyous wedding were in full swing. There was a festival kind of atmosphere, music was playing, and kids were dancing. Amidst the excitement, a unique condition emerged from the bride's father that seemed to threaten the harmony of the upcoming union of two families and two villages. The condition was- "No Senior Person should be present at the wedding festivities."

You can imagine the perplexing situation. The entire village was in dilemma. However, an expected hero emerged in the form of the groom's grandfather, a wise and seasoned individual who had weathered many storms in his life.

"Worry no, my dear ones, I will manage this small hiccup." He reassured everyone. And asked them, "You just need to manage my presence there"

Though the groom's party was sceptical, but had no other choice or option other than to manage his presence. So they agreed to grandfather's proposal.

On the day if the event, as they approached the bride's village. There was grand welcome to the party and they settled down there. Before next ceremony there was a message from the father of the bride. There was a seemingly impossible task in the form of a message. The task- to fill the nearby river with milk.

The atmosphere grew tense, and young boys contemplated returning empty-handed. However, the hero, the grandfather, confident and with a victory smile on his face, stepped forward. To the surprise of young generations, he said, Boys, this is a very small problem and very simple to solve. No one could believe in him and almost lost all hope. But the grandfather, with a twinkle in his eyes, He asked the boys to send this message, "Sir, we are ready with milk. Please make your river empty by draining or removing water from it." The boys jumped with joy.

This response turned which was looking like an insurmountable problem into a moment of humour and wisdom. The message was received by the father of the bride. He recognized the presence of a senior person at the marriage party and satisfied with the respect shown happily allowed the event to proceed.

LESSON LEARNED

The lessons learned from the marriage tale is clear- effective communication is not just about conveying words. It's about understanding values, accepting challenges, and sometimes, resolving seemingly impossible issues with creativity and a dash of humor.

Takeaway Message: the wedding, which could have been marred by an unusual condition, turned into a celebration of not just the union of two souls but also the triumph of effective communication, respect for seniors and the timeless wisdom, of the elder generation.

EXERCISE

Please make small notes on the following-

A- Reflection on Values

B- Adaptability in Communication

C- Building Trust through Actions

D- Navigating Challenges Creatively and

E- Respecting Senior Members

I suggest taking some time and thinking about the following-

1- Can you recollect any situation where humor has diffused the tension?

2- How can these lessons learned from the story be applied in your own life? and

3- Think of a recent challenge you faced. How will you approach to the same problem if it happens tomorrow?

MEASURING AND CELEBRATING SUCCESS

Establishing key performance indicators and celebrating individual and collective achievements:

It should be of utmost priority to establish KPI before you move further. In the absence of KPI, it will be very difficult to measure and celebrate any success. Here are a few suggestive steps from me-

A- Define Success Metrics: this is the first step you need to take. There will be some individual goals and one common goal or we can say shared goals, and in the previous chapter, we have seen the advantages of aligning these individual and organizational goals. Metrics will help you to decide how success is to be monitored for each goal. Set KPI in the beginning to avoid any kind of ambiguity. There should be quantitative and qualitative metrics so you can manage progress and achievement.

B- Tools to track progress: you can use spreadsheets or other project management software. I suggest regular tracking of the progress toward their goals.

C- Reflection and Adjustment: it is important to reflect on progress and sometimes they have to adjust goals and they should be ready to act as per circumstances or because new information has been raised. So regular reassessment of goals and strategies will be key to the success.

D- Celebrating Milestones: everyone wants motivation and you as a leader should use this opportunity to celebrate small victories, milestones, improving in target metrics, or overcoming a significant obstacle. This act of recognizing and celebrating their success will keep your team highly motivated.

E- Feedback: I would suggest encouraging a culture of open feedback and recognition within the team and among peers. This may look small act but has a significant impact on boosting morale and fostering a supportive environment for goal achievement.

F- Learning from setbacks: each setback or failure teaches us a lesson. You should view setbacks as an opportunity for growth and learning. This may take time to understand by your team, but this mindset shift can be crucial for resilience and long-term success.

G- Recording of Success Stories: I would recommend documenting your success stories and also your team's success stories. Not only record it but also share it with others. You can use it as a case study in the future.

H- Continuous Improvement: success is not a one-time event. There is scope and opportunity to improve daily and this mindset of continuous improvement must be encouraged by you as a leader.

STORYTIME

Measuring and celebrating success is a tale of *'Akbar and Birbal'* and the four fools.

One day, Emperor Akbar was in a good mood and enjoying the sunlight on a cold day with his courtiers. Akbar was fond of riddles and puzzles and posed a question to his courtiers: "Who are the four biggest fools in the kingdom?" Although everyone there tried to impress Emperor Akbar with their answers, he was not satisfied with any of them.

Then Birbal, Akbar's trusted advisor renowned for his wit and intelligence, stepped forward and presented a solution that intrigued the Emperor. Birbal proposed that the four fools in the kingdom were those who didn't know how to celebrate other's success.

To demonstrate his point, Birbal arranged a grand celebration in honor of a poor farmer who had harvested an unusually bountiful crop season. The farmer was overwhelmed by the recognition and gratitude shown by the Emperor and his court.

Impressed by Birbal's insight, Akbar realized the importance of celebrating the success of others. He decreed that henceforth, festivals would be organized throughout the kingdom to celebrate the achievements of farmers, artisans, and other common people.

Can we take a few key points as principles to be applied in your organization or within your team?

Celebrating Other's Success: a team leader as an individual and organization should cultivate a culture of appreciation and celebration for the success of their peers and colleagues.

In the past, we used to hold a celebration every three months during our quarterly meetings. Everyone looked forward to this event. During the celebration, I would give a memento to the wife of each individual. I did this to promote happiness and a sense of belonging among them.

Empathy: Learning from Birbal's actions demonstrates empathy towards the farmer, recognizing the hard work and dedication that led to his success. As someone who has worked with sales teams for many years, I have experienced extreme temperatures ranging from 2 degrees Celsius to over 46 degrees Celsius. This experience has been invaluable and worth millions of other rewards. Once you put your hand on someone's shoulder and say, 'I can understand', you create a place in their heart for the rest of their life. I suggest encouraging team leaders to empathize with others and show kindness and support in both their successes and failures.

Leading by example- You have a leadership role and should set an example by promoting a culture of appreciation and celebration.

Birbal's celebration offers a great advantage - Team Building. It fosters a sense of community and unity among the people of the kingdom. You get an opportunity to come together and celebrate shared success, which strengthens bonds and fosters a spirit of collaboration. It instills a feeling of "One Team, One Goal" in everyone.

Since we have been doing such activities every quarter and for many years, So I have learned a few lessons, and some experience to share with you on the subject of measuring and celebrating success. My father's advice to develop a habit of giving and you can start by giving thanks, showing gratitude etc became very useful.

At the celebration, several people were invited to share their thoughts and express their excitement about their success. Our team has developed a habit of expressing gratitude for their achievements and the support they received along the way. Even now, I can vividly picture those happy and satisfied faces.

"The celebrations we've had have been incredibly helpful for me and my team. They've allowed us to set new goals and increase our bar of success consistently without any feelings of distress or dissatisfaction. We always set a new goal once we've achieved a milestone, which keeps us motivated and forward-thinking. As a result, we've been able to ensure continued growth and progress."

At a later time, my mentor encouraged me to introduce an internal newsletter that featured a variety of success stories, personal experiences, and interviews with team members and their families. It's easy to imagine how this new approach transformed the workplace into one with a highly motivated team and outstanding performance.

Each celebration brought new opportunities, challenges, and responsibilities. Personally, I gained a lot from these events, which allowed me to experience personal growth and a deeper appreciation of success. They also provided valuable insights for future endeavors.

My father always guided me to stay grounded and humble even in the face of great success and I always practiced this and shared the same with my team leaders not to forget these invaluable lessons in their life.

My father always used to say, "Balance celebration and humility." Be open to new learning, be there with the team, and support others willingly on their path to success. Give credit for my success to my team.

I recall one of my interactions with my father back in March, just before the festival of "Holi" - a festival that celebrates colors. I had returned from a meeting and found that there was a celebration taking place. I was incredibly excited and shared many things with my father, who listened intently. After a while, he shared some words of wisdom with me, which I would like to pass on to you. These principles can serve as a guide for life.

1- Don't compare yourself to Others- each person's journey is unique, and success should be measured against personal goals and aspirations rather than external benchmarks.

2- Don't overlook Small Wins- "He noticed even the smallest things and was amazed. He said you missed opportunities to appreciate many people and their contributions." He quoted from Ramayana, The contribution of a squirrel in building a bridge when Shree Ram was going to attack Lanka.

3- Don't become complacent he warned me against becoming complacent upon reaching a milestone. He said, "Success should be viewed as a catalyst for further growth and advancement " After a pause he completed his sentence by saying- "rather than endpoint".

When I learned that he was noticing even small things from my talking, I was really curious and requested more insights, on what should I avoid or not to practice.

He suggested the following on my request-

4- Don't Ignore feedback and don't miss any learning opportunities. His advice was feedback is to be taken as an opportunity for improvement and growth.

5- Don't Celebrate at the expense of Others- celebrate your success with humility and sensitivity. Never diminish the achievement of others. celebration must be inclusive and respectful of the efforts and accomplishments of everyone involved.

6- Don't focus only on external validation- this piece of advice was a great source of my motivation- True success and fulfilment come from within, rooted in personal values, purpose, and intrinsic motivation, and not to seek validation and approval solely from external sources.. Awards and recognition are external validation.

7- Don't neglect self-care- his suggestion to me was to prioritize rest, relaxation, and self-reflection to recharge and maintain balance amidst the excitement of success.

8- Don't lose sight of long-term goals- again he warned me against becoming too focused on short-term achievements at the expense of long-term goals. Celebrations should be aligned with overarching objectives and values, ensuring continued progress and fulfilment in the future.

Before I left my father's place, he shared the following story about my neighbor's son.

In my village, there lived a man named Sevak. He was known for his ambition and love for celebrations. Sevak had a peculiar habit of throwing extravagant parties even for the smallest achievements. People admired him, but he spared no expense in celebrating his triumphs. According to my father, Sevak's brother tried to stop him from doing such silly things, but he successfully ignored that advice.

Sevak's reputation for throwing parties grew, and so did his debts. Luckily, his brother separated himself from the burden of any such debts. He was not even a guarantor of his debts. Sevak was borrowing money from anyone willing to lend, confident that his next success would bring him enough wealth to repay his loans. However, Sevak's luck eventually ran out when he failed to achieve the significant milestone he had been boasting about for months.

With creditors knocking on his door and no means to repay his debts, Sevak found himself in a dire situation. He was desperate for a solution and sought my advice. My father told me that he called Sevak and his brother and advised Sevak to celebrate his success but to avoid overindulgence and extravagance. He also asked Sevak whether he had any friends who could support him in this situation. My father told Sevak that true success isn't measured by the size of the party or the grandeur of celebration but by the meaningful impact of his achievements.

Sevak's brother helped him in his tough time, and Sevak vowed to be more mindful of his expenses and to celebrate success in moderation. Thanks to the timely intervention and help of his brother, Sevak's life was saved, and he gradually regained the trust and respect of the villagers.".

THE LESSON I LEARNED

While celebrating success is important, it's essential to avoid excessive spending and overindulgence. True success is not measured by material possessions or extravagant parties but by the meaningful impact of our achievements.

EXERCISE

Please list your 3 key takeaways as action points that you would like to implement in your Organization.

Please list 2 points that you want to avoid for yourself and your team.

CASE STUDY

I take this opportunity to share one real-time case study:

One of my friends joined a Pharma company as General Manager and his mandate was to bring the company to the growth phase. The company had registered negative growth in the last two financial years. Employee morale was low and management was ready to support a new leader to bring positive changes to the company. We discussed many aspects and helped my friend to find out the real cause of this negative growth.

We discussed in detail and agreed to these points-

1- Identify Problem

2- Validate your assumptions

3- Brainstorming for solutions within, and

4- Plan to implement actions

He did route cause analysis by using a fishbone diagram, also known as Ishikawa diagram or cause–and–effect diagram. Personally, I call it why –why technique to find route cause.

A fishbone diagram is a visual tool used to systematically identify potential root causes of a problem or issue. This tool was developed by Japanese quality control expert Karou Ishikawa in 1960. This tool is widely used in various industries for problem-solving and process improvement.

Just for your reference I am sharing the diagram

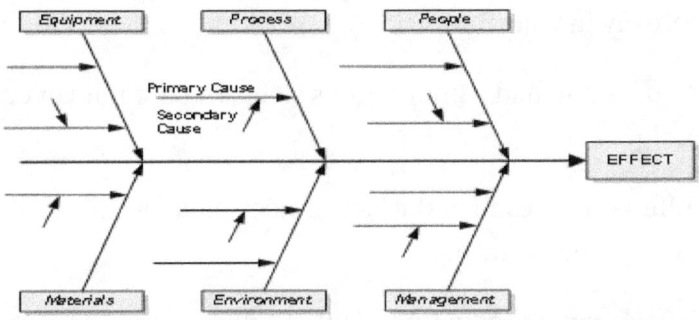

Let me help you to understand this better, as you may want to use this tool in your current role. The above, basis illustration shows the "head" of the fish representing the problem or effect, with "bones" branching out to represent different categories of potential causes.

If you are in process management or in the production department then branches can be as

Manpower, Machine, Material, Measurement, Methods and Mother Nature (Environment)

Since I am sharing a case study from the point of a Pharma professional, I am sharing categories relevant to him. For example- "People", "Process", Resources, etc.

There are primary causes and also can be secondary causes as well.

For example- "Lack of Sleep and Decreased Productivity" in this case Lack of Sleep is cause

And Decreased Productivity is the effect.

Let me explain one more step so you can use it more effectively in your field.

Cause- You had a poor night's sleep and did not get enough rest.

Effect- As a result of the lack of sleep, you feel tired and have difficulty concentrating.

Effect- your productivity at work decreases because you're unable to focus and complete tasks efficiently.

We met after a few years and he got his promotion within the same organization and his team was doing good. So I got an opportunity to learn about his journey. He shared a few things that have helped his team and brought success to their organization.

In his own words: I made a point on day 1 of my joining to my core team that let us forget past performance and share key learnings and what we want to achieve.

I used the why-why technique to find the root cause of the problem that led to employee dissatisfaction and disengagement. Once we reached a conclusion after this brainstorming then we agreed on what we will do and what we will avoid.

My 1st focus point was employee engagement and process rigor in the field operations and not on results. We decided to start a quarterly Award Ceremony for field people that included front-line managers too. Criteria were simple, "employees will nominate their peers for recognition on outstanding performance, and managers will validate and support with their efforts data." The idea was to give an opportunity to the team to demonstrate the company values. At the end of each quarter, the company hosted an awards ceremony where we used to put up banners with photographs of all nominated employees. We designed awards in various categories, for example- employee of the quarter for overall performance. Innovation award, the award for process champion, there was an award for team collaboration that improved relationships with team members and encouraged open communication with their team leaders.

Reward and Incentive: in addition to the above, recipients were given gift cards, a personalized trophies. This plan motivated my employees to strive for excellence and contributed to a positive work environment. There were other team-building activities planned by the product management team to keep them engaged. I made a point to invite the star performer with his family for dinner with me at their station, so I was making my work plan accordingly.

In addition to quarter awards, I introduced yearly awards for the top 10 employees in the company. That award included extra vacation days for them with their wives within the country.

The results:

Increased morale of the employees, everyone feeling valued and that brought job satisfaction in them. This program encouraged teamwork and collaboration as there were recognizing and celebrating each other's contributions. This recognition and celebration led to enhanced productivity and performance levels. My program contributed to a positive company culture characterized by mutual respect, support, and a shared sense of achievement.

"And above all, as shared above, I got a promotion"

EXERCISE

If you were in his place, then what have you done differently?

What would you like to do more for your teams?

With thanks to my friend for sharing his success story, I advise you to plan your success journey. "Your future should be shining brighter than your yesterday"

Let us move on to our next chapter to see how to tackle failures.

LEARNING FROM FAILURE

KEY LESSONS LEARNED

Embracing failure as a part of the goal-setting journey!

"Failure is not the opposite of Success it's part of success."

- Ariana Huffington

"Many of life's failures are people who did not realize how close they were to success when they gave up."

-Thomas Edison

Embracing Failure as a Stepping Stone to Success-

Can you recall the experience when you tried to ride a bicycle for the first time?

How excited you were! What was your determination to ride, and how was the initial wobbly ride? Learning to ride a bicycle is a universal experience that offers valuable insights into the process of learning from failure.

AN UNSTEADY START

imagine your childhood, filled with excitement as you hop onto your brand-new bicycle, ready to explore the world with your new wheels. You push off, feeling the rush of freedom, but suddenly find yourself going off course, with your pedals spinning widely, before crashing to the ground in a heap of limbs and scraped knees. Enjoying those memories! Isn't it? What were those days? Oh my God, you are missing those days as I am missing. Let me ask you a question,

What did you do, when you had such a painful experience? If say you were a failure in your attempt to ride a bicycle, would you agree? Of course you will not. Even though your first attempt at riding ends in failure, it doesn't dampen your enthusiasm at all. Rather you were more determined this time. in fact the level of enthusiasm was even more high that time. if I say that was an initial setback, you may agree, because you pick yourself up, dust off and wipe away tears, and climb back onto the saddle. How are you feeling now! Every further attempts, gave you more balance and confidence, despite experiencing more spills along the way. Each fall means, something new teaching! You learned with each such fall, how to steer, brake, and most importantly, how to get back up and try again. Very rightly said by Jack Canfield-"*It's not how far you fail, but how high you bounce that counts*"

Shall we say- it was falling forward. I would like to call it The Power of Persistence.

Let me ask you one more question here, were you not Finding a Balance?

"*Falling forward and trying to find the right balance is true learning from mistakes!*"

"As you continued to practice for more hours each day, you discovered that failure is not a sign of weakness but a necessary part of the learning process. You were cautious at every speed breaker, adjusting your approach by slowing down sometimes and increasing speed at other times. Slowly but surely, your wobbly rides transformed into smooth and confident glides."

Finally, it was The Triumph of Success:

Can you recall that magical moment, it Happened -you find your balance, your rhythm, your flow. The bicycle became an extension of yourself, effortlessly propelling you forward with each turn of the pedals. Can I say- **you have mastered the art of bicycling, not in spite of your failures, but because of them!**

This experience of learning to ride a bicycle is not just a childhood memory; it is a metaphor for life's journey. There were obstacles and setbacks but you overcame these setbacks and obstacles on your path to success.

Embrace failure as a teacher, a guide, and a catalyst for growth, and

Remember- The Journey is just beginning.

I am sharing a real-time case study and this case will give you an idea about the fall, the reason behind the fall, and their Rise again to the peak.

Ramdas Shared one story that was from his owner where he was serving as his driver.

It was around early 1990 and I was planning to start a small business in my city. I was with my father to seek his advice and blessings. Ramdas was there and he shared the following story.

There was a family-run business which was going well and the firm was enjoying great reputation. Three brothers were running this business. They were managing business in harmony and everyone was managing everything together. This means there was no clarity of their responsibilities. As time passed, the business began to face difficulties such as losing its customers and experiencing financial troubles.

The Fall- As the business experienced a decline, it became evident that it had a financial crunch. The eldest brother had a good friend who was a bank employee. One day he called his friend the eldest brother to his place, it was Sunday so I was also there. He suggested conducting a root cause analysis to identify the underlying issues responsible for the company's decline. His simple suggestion was to meet with loyal customers in person to comprehend their worries and reasons for the weakening relationship.

Analysis- The elder brother met a few of his loyal customers, collected information, and made a thorough analysis. It became evident that one of the primary reasons for the downturn was the deteriorating relationship; with customers. The younger brother lacked the essential skills and often displayed arrogance towards clients. As a result, this behaviour led to a loss of trust and loyalty among the customer base.

Strategic Changes- based on analysis his friend, a bank employee, suggested restructuring the roles of three of them. It was based on the strengths and weaknesses of each brother.

The junior brother, whose customer management skills were lacking, was reassigned to handle dispatch, and inventory management, roles that better suited his strengths.

Second brother, who excelled in accounts, took over the management of banking and cash transactions, and balance sheets to ensure financial stability.

The elder brother, resumed his role in customer relations and operations, leveraging his humility and customer-centric approach to build trust and loyalty.

Result- the strategic changes implemented by the elder brother quickly yielded positive results. By focusing on improving customer relations and streamlining short periods, the company once again emerged as a leading distributor in the town.

I asked Ramdas, what about you? With a smile on his face said, "Good Increment and special Deewali Bonus that year"

Lesson Learned:

Prioritizing customer relations and addressing customer concerns is crucial for business success.

Recognizing individual strengths and weaknesses and assigning roles accordingly can optimize team performance.

Being willing to adapt and make strategic changes is essential for overcoming challenges and staying competitive in the market.

By addressing the root cause and making strategic changes, you can overcome adversity and emerge stronger than before.

I used my learnings in my professional life and have witnessed great success to my team.

Our discussion so far has been centered around learning from failure and how to bounce back. One important element in staying motivated is the ability to sustain motivation while continuing to grow. Let's delve deeper into this topic.

SUSTAINING MOTIVATION

MAINTAINING ENTHUSIASM TO SUSTAIN LONG-TERM MOTIVATION

"When you have a dream, you have got to grab it and never let go."

- Carol Burnett

Let us talk about motivation first. Then we will talk about the importance of motivation in achieving goals.

In simple terms, motivation is identifying your motive and then taking action, so

Motivation is Motiv**e**+ A**c**tion. Remember e and c are silent here in this equation.

So motivation can be a force behind their actions for someone. Motivation is like seasons; summer, and winter, every year it comes and goes. So what will help you to sustain your motivation? There are many ways to keep you motivated and my suggestion has always been very simple to my team, it was- first identify your motive and take action, then help people to identify their motive and encourage them to take action.

Let me take you to the memory lane of my childhood one more time.

One Day Ramdas came to my father (his Guru Ji) with a feeling of low and doubt on his face. My father asked Ramdas about his well-being and offered him a glass of buttermilk.

Ramdas said, Guru Ji, I am not feeling good and not able to concentrate on my job. My owner is also not very happy with my work, So, I requested them for a break of two days.

My father asked Ramdas, what is your issue, what is bothering him so much? Ramdas, said, Guru JI, I have an offer to join one of my family friend's owner as his driver at Mumbai. I have been offered a good salary hike and promised of a good life. So what is an issue in this case Ramdas, Asked his Guru Ji to him. Ramdas continued, Guru Ji, my current employer is also like a family to me. They are taking good care of me, provided good accommodation, and takes care of me. Even yesterday, when I asked for a break, without asking any questions I was been given a break.

After a few moment's silence, my father told a story from the epic Mahabharata. The scene from the battlefield of Kurukshetra. As a small boy, I was wondering why is he telling him a story to Ramdas, when he was feeling so low. But somehow, I could resist. My father continued, Ramdas- I can understand you are grappling with doubts and uncertainties about your path forward. When I look back today I realize the point of my father, as he never was conclusive of anything, and was helping people to get the best answer to their questions themselves. He was trying to find if Ramdas was truly following his passion or merely pursuing success for the sake of societal expectations.

My father continued. Arjuna was a great warrior and one day he was facing crisis within himself. Crisis of motivation and purpose on the battlefield. He questioned Lord Krishna about the righteousness of his actions and the path laid out before him. Arjun was sceptical. He saw his own family before him and he has to win the war against them. He must defeat them and kill them. Arjuna continued, how can I attempt to kill my own Guru, and above all Pitamah Bhisma. Even if I win this war, but how can I relish even the kingdom of heaven without his family and Guru? What will he get by killing my family members? A piece of land? Lord Krishna, acting as Arjuna's charioteer, imparted the timeless teachings of the Bhagvad Gita, offering guidance on duty (Dharma), righteousness, and the nature of self.

Lord Krishna encouraged Arjuna to rise above his doubts and fulfill his sacred duty as a warrior, fighting not out of desire for victory or personal gain, but out of devotion to his duty and adherence to righteous action.

Ramdas Said, Guru Ji, I got the answer to my problem and my dilemma. I will follow my principles and not money.

I learned a few lessons that day –

1- One should understand his duty (Dharma)- What is the duty or purpose of one's life!

2- Stay Focused – Despite facing doubt and hesitation, Arjuna learned the importance of maintaining focus and resolving the pursuit of his goals.

3- Finding Inner Peace- Through self-awareness understand the nature of self and learn to find inner peace and stability.

4- Sustain Motivation- The teaching of the Bhagavad Gita serves as a source of inspiration and motivation for Arjuna and today to all of us, helping sustain the commitment to his duty even in the face of challenges and adversity.

If I take this story and compare it with the corporate world then I can say- your duty is not just to excel in your job or climb the corporate ladder. It is to uphold your values, follow your passion, and make a meaningful impact in the world around you. Stay true to your principles, and success will follow.

Remember- "The true fulfillment comes not from external accolades or material success, but from living authentically and aligning your actions with his deepest values"

FINDING THE PURPOSE IN ADVERSITY

You will grow stronger, wiser, and more resilient, embodying the timeless teaching of the Bhagavad Gita in your personal and professional life.

Another way to sustain motivation could be – **"Finding the Purpose in adversity"**

Let me share the life experience of one of my friend's sons, who was a bright and ambitious young man, eager to make his mark in the corporate world. Fresh out of college, got a job at a prestigious multinational company, filled with joy, enthusiasm, and dreams. He joined the job in the city of Bengluru and very soon he was selected as a Team lead for an international customer. He was a dedicated, disciplined boy. He tackled new customer so well with zeal, eager to prove himself and climb corporate ladder. His hard work paid off, and was promoted to junior management position, overseeing a team of his own.

Then soon after: he began to feel overwhelmed by the demands and pressures of management. He started questioning his abilities and suitability for the job. The once-promising young man now found himself struggling to cope with the responsibilities thrust upon him.

One Day- Feeling lost and disheartened he called his father over phone. He poured out his frustration, sharing his fears of failure and inadequacy.

The Wisdom of his Father (My Friend)- he listened patiently to his son's concerns. His father did not say anything about the management or his team , rather told him a story of **Arjuna** from **Bhagavad Gita**. My friend confronted his son with doubts and uncertainties. His son got clarity of purpose, and the strength to fulfil his duty as a warrior (Like **Arjuna** got Clarity from Lord **Krishna**)

After a few months, I met them at their residence in Mumbai and his son shared the following.

I realized that my struggles were not unique. Like many others I too faced challenges and I could get timely guidance from my father like Arjuna got from Lord Krishna. I could draw strength from within and find my purpose in the face of adversity. I embraced my challenges as opportunities for growth.

I am happy to share with you that today he is working in a senior leadership position and is doing great.

These timeless principles of duty, motivation, and self-discovery will inspire you to sustain your motivation.

What else can sustain my motivation? I was always looking for the answer to my question and I got many suggestions from my mentor and my friends. I found in my life Goal setting itself brings motivation and clarity of goals help in sustaining motivation.

GOAL SETTING

"If you want to be happy, set a goal that commands your thoughts, liberates your energy and inspires your hopes."

*– **Andrew Carnegie***

Goal setting and motivation are closely related with each other. One day my father called me and brothers and asked a question, " What you want to achieve in your life?" he gave us one day to think and comeback with our answers. His suggestion was to have our own goal and also why of that Goal?. Though I was very young at that time but a few things I can recall even today, when we met next day with our sheets.

My father's first lesson to us was- to set clear and specific goals, and also why.

To answer my question, he narrated a story from the epic Mahabharata, it was the story of *"Ekalavya."*

STORYTIME

Ekalavya was a talented and determined archer who aspired to master the art of archery under the guidance of the renowned guru, Dronacharya. He approached guru Dronacharya with his request seeking his mentorship. His request was turned away by Dronacharya, by saying, " he was committed to teaching only the prices of Kuru dynasty".

Ekalavaya was determined to achieve mastery in archery so he was undeterred by this rejection. He fashioned a clay image of Dronacharya as his guru and started practicing tirelessly, honing his skills and perfecting his technique.

As time passed, his dedication and skill as an archer surpassed even that of the Kuru Princes who had been privileged to train under guru Dronacharya. One Dronacharya came across Ekalavya practicing his archery with remarkable precision and prowess.

Impressed by Ekalavya's skill Dronacharya approached him and asked about his guru. Ekalayva proudly pointed to the clay image of Dronacharya, declaring him to be his guru. Dronacharya realized that Ekalavya was better than his own disciples in archery despite never having received formal training from him.

With this story, he took a break and I with my brothers were finding place to hide, no one was having such specific goal as Ekalavaya had- to become a master archer.

Key words were – Passion, Determination, Focus, and dedication for success

Through this story we learn the importance of setting clear and specific goals.

I learned that day from my father that once we are progressing towards and accomplishing goals instills a sense of achievement in us and bring satisfaction. Not only this once you accomplish your goals your confidence goes high, your self-esteem improves. When I grew and became a sales professional then I realized that my efforts and perseverance made to set more ambitious and relevant goals.

Remember: **"Ambitious goals are those that stretch individuals beyond their current capabilities and comfort zone"**

Having clear and specific goals has several benefits, one of which is the ability to measure progress and track success. In addition, if there are any deviations or adjustments required, you can check your performance against specific metrics and milestones. This helps you stay on track and achieve your goals efficiently and effectively.

Accountability: Specific goals create accountability in us. You feel accountable for your actions and you will not hesitate to ask for help and support and also seek feedback from others to improve outcomes.

Results: Clear and specific goals increase the likelihood of success. Once you are clear about what is expected of you or what you expect from yourself, you prepare well and are ready to face any challenges and overcome any obstacle.

Goal Setting: Focus on Process, as guided by Ashim Sarmah, "Focus on the process more than the goal; goal leads to success or failure, the process leads to the goal"

I would like to take a break here and before I say good luck for a successful journey and for being a great leader, let me share a story to conclude this episode.

It was election time in my village for the head of the village and I still was growing and was in the village only, when I left my village to study in the city, I was at the age of 14 years, so it was around that time. Ramdas decided to fight the election that year and he was highly charged as he was a natural leader and was liked by many in the village, he came to his guru Ji (My Father) to seek his blessings and advise him to move on to file his papers. It was around 8 PM and vividly I remember their discussion. It goes ....

My father asked Ramdas a few questions, why do you want to fight this election? What is your vision for your village's progress? Do you have clear goals in your mind? Can you see those goals happening in the reality? Will you be able to align those goals with your values?

I remember the determination of Ramdas and requested Guru Ji, Can I come tomorrow morning with my answers to hour questions, I need to prepare well, Ramdas was very honest in his approach and accepted that Guru Ji, "I never knew that this role has so much of responsibilities with it". I agreed to his request.

I realized it was that evening Ramdas embarked on a transformative journey of self-discovery. He engaged himself in deep introspection and contemplation. He learned the timeless principles of goal-setting and mastery.

My father taught Ramdas the importance of Clarity in setting goals, just as a traveler needs a clear destination to reach his destination. And specific goals to guide his actions and decisions as a ruler. I along with Ramdas, learned the Significance of Aligning goals with one's core values and principles. True success and fulfillment come from pursuing goals that are in harmony with one's highest aspirations.

Another learning we got was the importance of courage and determination in pursuing ambitious goals. Ramdas understood that adversity and challenges are inevitable on the path to success. It requires one's perseverance that ultimately leads to triumph.

Ramdas did a thorough analysis of his strengths, and strengths of sitting village Head, his vision for the village, and his determination. He realized that the sitting head is a visionary leader, who can guide the villagers with wisdom, compassion, and purpose better than him. He decided to withdraw his name from fighting the election. Though he never fought election but was a clear winner in the eyes of everyone. I love You, Ramdas!

Suggestions:

Goal setting is a powerful process that enables individuals to clarify their aspirations, focus their efforts, and achieve meaningful outcomes. The process of goal setting involves several key steps:

Identify your goals- Begin by identifying SMART goals.

Create an Action Plan- Break down your goals into smaller, manageable tasks and create a detailed action plan. Outline the steps needed to accomplish each objective, and set timelines and milestones to track your progress along the way.

Stay Motivated- Cultivate intrinsic motivation by connecting your goals to your values, interests, and long-term aspirations. Visualize your success, celebrate your progress, and stay focused, and stay focused on the positive impact of achieving your goals.

Adapt and Adjust- Remain flexible and open to adjusting your goals and action plans as needed. Be open to learning from setbacks, and embracing new opportunities that arise along the way.

Seek Support and be Accountable- Surround yourself with a supportive network of friends, family, mentors, and peers who can offer encouragement, guidance, and accountability as you work towards your goals.

EXERCISE - REFLECTIVE GOAL-SETTING

What are your most important goals and aspirations in life?

Why are these goals meaningful to you?

How do they align with your values and passions?

What specific steps can you take to move closer to your goals? Break down your goals into smaller, accountable tasks.

What obstacles or challenges do you anticipate in pursuing your goals? How will you overcome them?

How will you stay motivated and focused on your goals?

Based on your reflections create a concrete action plan for goal achievement;

My suggestions-"Visit your goals regularly and monitor your progress towards your goals."

FINAL THOUGHTS

The process of goal-setting is not just about achieving a particular destination, but it is also about embracing the journey of growth, self-discovery, and self-mastery. As we ponder over the principles discussed in this book, we should remember the significant impact that intentional goal-setting can have on our lives.

Each goal we set becomes a stepping stone on our path to personal and professional fulfillment, guiding us toward a future filled with purpose, passion, and possibility.

So, as you embark on your journey of goal-setting and self-discovery, I encourage you to embrace the transformative power of intention, commitment, and action.

Remember- The greatest rewards often lie beyond our comfort zones, and that every challenge we encounter is an opportunity for growth and learning.

May you continue to pursue your goals with unwavering determination, resilience, and optimism, knowing that the seeds you plant today will blossom into a future of infinite potential and possibilities.

> "The future belongs to those who believe in the beauty of their dreams."
>
> *– Eleanor Roosevelt*

With, warm and best wishes for a true mastery of Goal Setting!

I remain yours Always!!

ABOUT THE AUTHOR

JP Pathak emerges as a seasoned professional in the realms of sales, management, training, and coaching, with a remarkable journey spanning over 35 years. As a dedicated student of sales and management, he has honed his expertise not only as a practitioner but also as a mentor, guiding individuals to discover their **"One Thing"** that propels them toward realizing their dreams and purpose.

Throughout his extensive career, JP has navigated the intricacies of sales and marketing, earning a reputation as a sales superstar in his own right.

One of JP's distinctive qualities lies in his ability to simplify complex concepts, making them accessible and understandable for his audience. His training and coaching methods are infused with a touch of humor, creating an environment that fosters relaxation and comfort, even in challenging situations or when dealing with difficult-to-manage individuals.

JP's effectiveness as a trainer is not solely based on his vast experience but is also enriched by his capacity to weave anecdotes and small stories into his teachings. These narratives serve as memorable lessons, ensuring that the knowledge imparted remains ingrained in the minds of his students for an extended period.

By incorporating humor and storytelling, JP not only imparts wisdom but also creates an engaging and enjoyable learning experience.

Beyond his professional endeavors, JP Pathak is a science graduate who shares his life with his wife and two daughters. His commitment extends beyond individual growth, as he actively contributes to the development of both people and organizations. Through his training and coaching initiatives, JP leaves an indelible mark on the journey of those he guides, fostering growth and success.

DISCLAIMER

This book is for informational purposes only. Readers acknowledge that the author does not render legal, financial, medical, or professional advice. The content within this book has been derived from various sources. Please consult a licensed professional before attempting any techniques outlined in this book.

By reading this document, the reader agrees that under no circumstances is the author responsible for any direct or indirect losses incurred as a result of the use of the information contained within this document, including but not limited to errors, omissions, or inaccuracies. Adherence to all applicable laws and regulations, including international, federal, state, and local governing professional licensing, business practices, advertising, and all other jurisdictions, is the sole responsibility of the purchaser or reader. Neither the author nor the publisher assumes any responsibility or liability whatsoever on behalf of the purchaser or reader of these materials. Any perceived slight of any individual or organization is purely unintentional.

MAY I ASK YOU A FAVOR?

At the outset, I want to give you a big thanks for reading this book. You could have chosen any other book, but you took mine, and I appreciate this. I hope you have at least a few actionable insights that will positively impact your daily life.

Can I ask for 30 seconds more of your time?

I'd love it if you could leave a review of the book. That will help me grow my readership by encouraging folks to take a chance on my books.

Keeping it straight - *reviews are the lifeblood of any author.*

It will take less than a minute of your time but will tremendously help me reach out to more people. **Kindly provide your review at the store you bought this book from.** And I'd love to see your review. Thanks for your support.

www.ingramcontent.com/pod-product-compliance
Lightning Source LLC
Chambersburg PA
CBHW070151230526
45471CB00002B/610